Drawing and Painting

ARCHITECTURE
IN LANDSCAPE

Drawing and Painting

ARCHITECTURE
IN LANDSCAPE

ADRIAN HILL
V.P.R.O.I., R.B.A.

BLANDFORD PRESS

DEDICATION

DORRIE AND CLEM PRICE THOMAS

with Affection

© *Blandford Press Ltd*, 1966
167 High Holborn, London, WC1

First published 1966
Printed in Great Britain by
Jarrold and Sons Ltd, Norwich

Title page photograph by Keystone

Contents

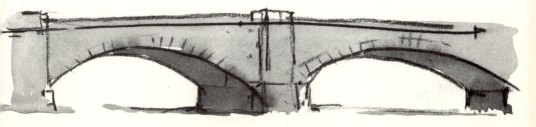

Introduction

LET me reassure the reader at the outset that the title of this little book is not addressed to the potential perspectivist nor to the student of architecture, but only to the student of landscape painting who is interested in the relationship of architecture to Nature and who wishes to introduce man-made structures, ancient and modern, as motifs for his outdoor compositions.

If this be the case the reader has the right to ask whether perspective is of primary importance to its achievement. The answer is both "yes" and "no" according to the student's approach. To the further question "Is a knowledge of architecture necessary?" the answer again must be the same.

For surely it goes without saying that whatever be the subject of our choice, whether it be portraits, animals, trees or flowers, the more we know about their origin and construction, the better chance we will have of investing our pictures with authority—correctly as well as artistically! The two aims must develop together, if their final presentation is to be acceptable.

Moreover, the subject of this book is rightly concerned with fundamental problems, such as optical principles, which include picture plane and viewpoints, for these will be found to be the truths (or rules) by which we are best able to see and depict our chosen basic structures in their landscape setting. Within these terms of reference, an additional aim of the following chapters will be to reintroduce the reader to a somewhat neglected pictorial acquaintance in the hope that it will ripen into a fruitful partnership, whereby architecture may again offer exciting forms both old and new with which to enliven the contemporary landscape. With regard to the illustrations, I have resisted the temptation to supply too many ready-made subjects as portrayed in guide-books, which focus mainly on historic landmarks—ecclesiastic or domestic—for the edification of the visitor.

But rather the reader may pick and choose from the avowedly

mixed bag of architectural offerings I have discovered in sketching grounds of my own choosing. For personal enterprise is far more rewarding than obedience to directions and one's own personal compass preferable to that offered by an official courier or signpost.

Inherent in the problem of adopting this method is the possibility that my examples may seem less than worthy of their subject.

Beethoven once hoped that "what comes from the heart goes to the heart", and although hearts are notoriously unpredictable organs, the illustrations I have ventured to select from my own sketch-books must stand as witness of my own pleasure—and I hope profit—in the pursuit of this branch of landscape painting, and will perhaps rekindle a desire in the reader to obtain a similar measure of enjoyment.

I have, for considerations of space, limited my own drawings to that offered by architecture found in the countryside of Great Britain. To cover anything approaching the range and variety of characteristic buildings indigenous to the terrain of foreign countries would fill more books than a single volume could possibly contain.

The four types of architecture which we shall be considering under the title of this work fall under the following headings:

Domestic: Every kind of dwelling place in urban and country districts.

Devotional: Cathedrals, churches, manor-houses, etc.

Memorial: All historic monuments.

Civil: Every edifice built for commerce or pleasure.

BELLINI *The Madonna of the Meadow*
Reproduced by courtesy of the Trustees, The National Gallery, London

CHAPTER ONE

Down the Ages

ARCHITECTURE, strictly speaking, only concerns the painter when the building incorporates in its construction some feature, or features, not essential to its basic purpose but in its setting pleases or impresses the eye. In this way we are impressed with its grace or mightiness as in a cathedral or castle, or receive aesthetic enjoyment from the enrichment of detail or costly materials, as in some historic house, or in a lesser degree with the half-timbered façade, the interplay of vertical and horizontal beams with the decorated gables and windows in the humbler scale of our cottage dwellings.

As in previous books in this series, let us then first take a look at the past and see what part architecture has played in the composition of the Old Masters' landscapes of both British and foreign schools. With very few exceptions there is abundant proof in our national collections that at one time or another these painters have all seized on the architectural feature to be found in the countryside. All have made pictorial use of man-made structures and all have painted them with an eye for their artistic value in their landscape compositions, and have integrated them each in their particular fashion. Indeed, I would say that something architectural to offset Nature appeared indispensable to the attainment of this end. (That and with the knowledge that if this architectural ingredient added a pictorial flavour to satisfy the artistic appetite of the art lover and made the picture more—dare I say—marketable—it is surely understandable!) Admittedly in many cases the chosen cottage, castle or church is but a small incident in the picture; but just how important it is—only by its absence from the scene is the lack made manifest. However distant the feature may be in the painting, without it the focal point of interest would be missing. All down the ages, buildings of every description have been utilized to contrast with and complete Nature's setting. One to counterbalance the other. This is understandable when one reflects that Nature in her natural state is mainly fashioned in the round. She follows rhythmic lines, sweeping this way and that, turns upon herself, rises and falls, advances and retreats in something of the same way as her close relation, the sea. Moreover, Nature is ever imprecise, ever on the move, is never absolutely static and on the stillest of days remains animated in repose. It is her lasting charm.

In contrast, the building, having no organic life of itself, remains stubbornly rooted in the earth and has (unless completely covered with ivy) a hard and cutting edge to its shape; it could be said to be impervious to Nature's machinations.

The so-called personality of a great house functions inside its four walls which contain, like a suit of armour as it were, the warrior inside! Whatever life and drama is enacted within, the façade remains obdurately the same. If the exterior form can be said to "live", it is the stoic solidity of the fabric that proclaims itself with man-made dignity, even with a measure of arrogance, as if to say, "Look at me, admire my strength. I never bend or bow or shake—or flutter! How valiantly I stand inviolate among all this changing restless vegetation."

COROT *The Roman Campagna, with the Claudian Aqueduct*
Reproduced by courtesy of the Trustees, The National Gallery, London

Four-square, uncompromising, uncomplaining and often lonely, the man-made monument is seen to improve with the passage of years and when at last it slowly crumbles into decay, still remains aloof and distinct from its volatile surroundings. Even when man has hastened its destruction as was seen in the shattered towns and villages in two world wars, the tortured and distorted fabric in its very death-throes has presented a new and tragic aspect of its hazardous existence which made it pictorially very effective.

No wonder the Old Masters, in times of peace and plenty and surrounded by so much architectural beauty with so little of ugliness (or so it seems now), seized eagerly upon the building of the period and used it to such good effect.

Certainly the appeal of their landscapes would fall short in the eyes of the art lover without some architecture to supplement the scene. As far back as the fifteenth century, Giovanni Bellini in such religious paintings as his *The Madonna of the Meadow* introduced a fortified house and farm buildings to support the figure composition of the Virgin and Child, as did Veneziano in *The Miracle of St. Zenobious*, and Tintoret in his painting of St. George and the Dragon. Guardi and Canaletto specialized in the architectural motif. Stone, timber, brickwork tiles are alike rendered with a perfect comprehension of their relative qualities and are all demonstrated with great dexterity, as is seen in the latter's famous painting, *The Stone Mason's Yard* (National Gallery). Indeed Canaletto, even when he came to England, painted townscapes rather than landscapes. In Florence we know that perspective and mathematics were studied by such painters as well as the problems of representation, proportion and disposition of buildings. Moving from Italy to Holland and we see that Berchem, in addition to his paintings of Harlem, scores time after time by introducing ruins into his landscapes. Practically all Claude's magnificent paintings contain buildings—rustic as well as classic. Is it not the distant bridge in Corot's *The Claudian Aqueduct* that makes the scene so pictorially complete?

Best known as a painter of cattle, all Cuyp's landscape backgrounds will be seen to include a castle, a church or a windmill. While in all Heyden's landscapes, the architectural feature is dominant. In those paintings we possess of Hobbema, the homely cottage finds its rightful place, and in no work of Van der Neers is there lacking a building of some sort and this also applies to the landscapes of Poussin. Although at first sight the main interest

RUBENS *The Château de Steen*
Reproduced by courtesy of the Trustees, The National Gallery, London

of Rubens's notable picture is the vast panoramic view of the countryside, it is the manor-house on the right that gives it its title, *The Château de Steen*.

In the majority of Ruisdael's Nature paintings, churches, water-mills and ruined castles perform their pictorial role. And whenever Tenier ventures outside, some man-made structure is sure to appear in his paintings.

As we move forward to the landscapes of the Impressionists, we find them full of bridges, houses, taverns, windmills, churches and tumbledown cottages. Pissaro and Monet especially delighted in street scenes as did Utrillo and Sisley and, later, Cézanne. And surely nobody has painted rural architecture with more affection and intensity than Van Gogh, whether it be a canal, bridge, primitive homestead or the exterior of a brassy café.

What did he do as soon as he had moved into his humble home at Arles but hurry outside with his paints to record with pride the house in one of his most human and vigorous pictures.

Can we ever think of any landscape of Vlaminck without seeing the roadside cottage—or inn—painted with such swift and dramatic effect?

And when we come to our own British School, it is the architectural motif without which again and again their landscapes would lack substance and vitality. Take for example Turner's *Northam Castle* and Constable's *Hadleigh Castle*, and ask yourself whether Nature alone could have stood up as a composition without these dramatic ruins.

CONSTABLE *Hadleigh Castle*

While castles haunted Turner, Salisbury Cathedral served Constable for at least four of his famous landscapes. Turner in his peripatetic journeys round Great Britain and the Continent always sought out the architectural feature, as his sketch-books show. Constable, on the other hand, uses it whenever it suits his purpose and happens to occur in the scene, as the house and church in *The Glebe Farm*, or the bridge in *Helmincham Dell*, or Willy Lott's cottage as it appears in *The Haywain*. But when the great house was encountered such as *Malvern Hall* then it became the chief character in the scene, as it was the actual building which dominated the view and inspired the painting. Painters who followed and who utilized man-made structures—mills, bridges, castles or cottages—such masters as John Crome, Cotman, Samuel Palmer, David Cox and Peter de Wint take their rightful place in this review, for architecture of some sort is rarely absent from their landscapes.

McNeill Whistler, although coming as he does much later in our gallery, demonstrated his love of architecture in all his etchings of Venice and in the Thames-side series and he certainly made history when he exhibited his famous impression of *Battersea Bridge* which resulted in the libel case he bought against Ruskin and for which he was awarded a farthing damages! (Whistler claimed £1,000 libel damages against Ruskin for writing . . . "I have seen and heard much of Cockney impudence before now, but never expected to hear a coxcombe ask £200 for flinging a pot of paint in the public's face" (1878).) Among our more immediate contemporaries, admirable topographic landscapes have come from the pen, pencil and brush of Steer, Sickert, Muirhead Bone, Charles Cundall, Claude Muncaster, H. Workman, John Piper, Kenneth Rowntree, R. Badmin, Henry Rushbury and W. Fairclough, to name only a few. It would be interesting and instructive to continue this account because I believe this country has a monopoly in this representative type of landscape, most notably brought to light in the four volumes *Recording Britain*, in which the majority of illustrations bear witness to the importance attached to architecture in recording the countryside. However briefly, enough I hope, has been recalled to encourage the student to emulate the practice already established in this particular aspect of landscape painting and to continue the good work.

CHAPTER TWO

Cottages and Farmsteads

IN describing the charm of the English countryside, it is true to say that every village "has its giants as well as its dwarfs, its tritons as well as its minnows". All can boast of some historic building of the past as well as the humbler dwellings of the local inhabitants. Both types have their appeal though the castle is often a ruin and the house of state and power now no more than listed as an ancient monument. In the early part of this century, no country in the world possessed rural homes and villages which had the charm and picturesqueness of our own countryside and I believe in some measure this boast still holds good today. Thus, when we first venture out to prospect the country for something to sketch, there is probably no feature so much a natural part of the English landscape, nor one which makes such a direct appeal to the heart and our pen or brush, as the old country cottage.

Often heavily thatched and with small diamond-glassed windows, "their porches embroidered with honeysuckle and a bricked or tiled footway to the wicket gate" and a water butt crouched against the whitewashed wall, such picturesque and often outdated dwellings can still be met with on the outskirts of a town or village, or standing isolated on the moor or downs, still bearing witness to the enterprise, vision and pride of past stonemasons and carpenters. Indeed, no aspect of rural building is so full of surprises as the study of cottage architecture. In one village the cottages are of brick, in another of stone, in another half-timber and brick and thatch. These expressions, local and particular, have given to our villages their characteristic stamp. The use of the contrasting materials was probably due to the limited supply of a certain commodity. The practice of building cottages and farmhouses in clay dates back to the eighteenth century, and R. W. Brunskill tells us that over one hundred examples of clay-walled dwellings may still be seen on the Solway plain and were at one time common in parts of Cumberland. Many of them have since been rebuilt in stone and brick with some

elegance. Welsh slate predominates in roof covering with chimney-stacks in brick. Although rapidly dwindling in numbers these clay-faced cottages that still survive have a characteristic nature of their own and are well worth considering as pictorial features in a landscape. But there always remains the danger of stressing their very picturesqueness. Very few of these dwellings, by the way, are satisfactory by modern sanitary standards, but from the outside which is our concern, they have always exercised a compelling attraction for the artist, especially if the cottage is in a state of decay or near collapse!

In short the danger lies in their old world charm! However, there are still cottage properties which have a good design and a robust appearance. Homes of simple dignity, of right proportions, fabric and colour. Such harmonize with their surroundings and each county provides its quota which are characteristic of the local terrain. Either in their own right or seen in company with others by the roadside, they are all serviceable for our picture-making.

The homes of Lacock, though extremely attractive to look at from the road, stand much as they did in Tudor times. The National Trust has now embarked on the job of bringing the interiors up to date without disturbing the lovely grey exteriors. To find room for up-to-date plumbing, new dormer windows may have to be added in the same style as those built four hundred or more years ago.

It is an unobtrusive job with its own rewards that are seldom realized except by the painter and architect.

Suffolk Farm House

Cottage in Winchelsea, Sussex—carbon pencil and tint

Farmyard sketch

Examples showing variety of architectural detail

Cowdray Stables, Sussex

FARMSTEADS

Farmhouses, with their annexe of barns, granaries and stables, are traditionally popular for landscapes. They abound in most counties and are rich and varied in design. Either from a distance where they can be seen to settle snugly into the valley or straggle with artistic gait on the slopes of a hillside, or at close quarters, they offer ample material—not only in the farm outhouses, barns and haystacks themselves, but in a profusion of farm impedimenta—ploughs, harrows, tractors, harvest combines, not to mention cock and hens in the cobbled yard, pigs in their styes and ducks on the pond! And sometimes the old haywain, now a pensioner, can be seen taking its rest underneath a clump of trees. Like most artists, a farm draws me like a magnet and in this connection, the reader will find he is at liberty to roam where he pleases and draw what he wants—as long as he sees that all gates are securely latched on his departure! And what a variety of designs such gates and fences offer for separate study.

The temptation, as with the country cottage, is to over-sentimentalize the scene—to pick on the artistic disorder, to underline the out-of-date "lay-out" of the property, to overlay the purpose of the farm with a colourful cosiness derived from popular pictures of the past. It is rather with a modern rendering of the present-day aspects of the subject which will absolve our paintings from any such nostalgic overtones and present it acceptable to modern art requirements. In short, a well-ordered, up-to-date farm can furnish all the requirements of a well-ordered and composed contemporary painting!

Oasthouses in Kent. A pen-and-ink drawing showing decorative treatment

CHAPTER THREE

Exeter Cathedral

Cathedrals and Churches

ALTHOUGH this country may not perhaps be considered a particularly Christian one—in respect of church-going—it is certainly not for the lack of places of worship. Widely distributed throughout the length and breadth of Britain, every creed and denomination is catered for and in some localities, churches can be found standing almost shoulder to shoulder. Of the forty larger cities in England, Norwich surpasses all in the number of churches, containing no less than thirty-seven, all old and picturesque. For the artist, therefore, there is in every county plenty of ecclesiastical architecture to tempt his pencil and brush from the imposing and historic cathedral to the ancient and humbler village church, chapel or even meeting house.

Although a number of these were destroyed by enemy action in the last war, and others, being considered redundant, have been since pulled down or are under threat of demolition, additions to their depleted ranks are visible in many districts, not a few of them being of a distinctly modern design, notably those recently erected by the Roman Catholics. In past paintings the church has always found a place in the landscape and often been given pride of place, age adding a romantic appeal as well as a picturesque charm to most sacred buildings. Even for the worldly visitor as well as the artist, it is usual for his steps to be first directed to the church wherever it is to be found in the city, town or village that is visited. And it often transpires that it is the church that, once located, contains the necessary pictorial features for the artist's first sketch—or painting. Mainly this is due to its size, shape and outline of tower or

Fingest Church—Chilterns

Southwark Cathedral

Church in Wiltshire

spire. Because of these characteristics, a church stands sentinel, as it were, over the surrounding buildings. Benign, yet aloof, by nature of its special design and ancient lineage, it contrasts sharply with those adjacent domestic buildings with their humbler proportions and discrepancies in local colour. Moreover, it is these differences that establish the church's right to a place of honour—an honour which is seldom challenged and rarely usurped by Nature's forms.

Dumfries Abbey—Note the guide lines for proportion and composition

And especially is this pictorial domination true when from a distance it is often the cathedral that first proclaims the whereabouts of its name-place. As examples, mention should be made of Lincoln, Norwich, Salisbury, Ely, Litchfield, Chichester and the most recent at Guildford, where the outline of these cathedrals, their towers, and spires, first come into view and attract the eye with magnetic force. From this first distant sight, there are naturally a number of other aspects as we approach nearer to the cathedral or church and many of these viewpoints should be considered before we meet the edifice face to face where all its architectural features are fully disclosed. As a close-up our problem is to decide what we have to leave out! And here, lighting can help us. While a morning light will lay bare a uniformity of detail, a sinking sun will throw shadows, subduing many portions of the decorated façade and high-lighting others. Shadows can come to our rescue by transforming the surface of the fabric, by weaving a pattern of tone across a pillar and over a buttress—thereby heightening a sense of solidity and giving depth to the various facets of the structure.

A distinctive silhouette against the sky

24

From the unflinching grimness of the typical rural chapel to be found in Cornwall and Wales to the restraint and beautiful simplicity, say, of St. Mary's Stanstead in Kent, or the Anglo-Saxon style with its unusual tower-arch of St. Mary the Virgin at Sompting, Sussex, the unique grace and majesty of Thaxted Parish Church and the characteristic thatched-roofed churches to be found in Suffolk, it is hardly necessary to remind the reader of the abundant variety of church design, to be found in every corner of the country.

Special mention, however, should be made of some outstanding examples such as St. Peter and Paul at Lavenham in Suffolk. A truly majestic edifice, which, with the beautiful church which stands on the hill above the village of Kersey, are but two which this county can rightly boast of and many painters have done justice to. Tendring in Essex offers an imposing design in the form of St. Edmund's Church with its embattled tower and rounded steeple, while at Colchester in direct contrast the most unusual and paintable St. Mary's Church stands isolated in the meadows of Tilty. Another

Here the trees help to soften the outline

25

From highest steeple to humble gateway

26

Fernhurst Green—a study in chalk, watercolour and coloured pencil

Terrick Mill—final sketch (see preliminary sketches on p. 74)

Guide lines help to "hold together" the composition of a street scene.

The church dominates the village street

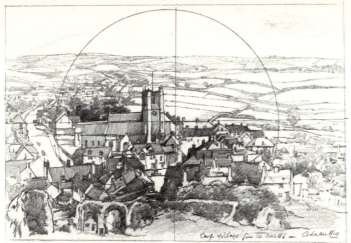

The drawing is more detailed in the focus of the picture.

Stratford-on-Avon in line and wash.

A wash used to emphasize evening light

Two impressions of Guildford Cathedral, Surrey

church with a number of irregular and interesting features especially in the round tower which catches the eye, is situated in the same county at Little Saling. And finally a notable example of East Anglian flint flush-work can be found in the parish church of Southwold, built probably by the wood merchants and farmers in the sixteenth and seventeenth centuries.

In Cheshire the spell of Gawsworth Church and manor is undeniable. No matter from which direction the church is approached, the subject is most paintable and is generally acclaimed by artists to be one of the most beautiful in England, presenting a combination of Art and Nature as every line of the historic building is reflected in the crystal waters of the foreground.

Holnest Church, dedicated to the Assumption of the Blessed Virgin—an unusual dedication in England—offers a most unique feature in its south wall, which is pierced with round-headed openings into the aisle. This, and with its fourteenth-century west tower with parapet and battlements and its fourteen external consecration crosses, makes it a "must" for the sketch-book.

Indeed, we are blessed with so many churches of great antiquity which all seem to cry out for a literal pictorial translation. In shape, size, colour and faultless proportions, it would seem to need but an accurate eye and a reverent hand to achieve the desired effect. But we must not be influenced too much by nostalgia but control our affection for their age and origin and concentrate on their picture qualities in terms of our chosen medium and seen through our own eyes as they appear in the light of the present-day conditions.

Castle and church—Corfe, Dorset

31

CHAPTER FOUR

Castles

CASTLES, other than those like Corfe in Dorset and Bamber in Sussex, which like others are now no more than veritable ruins, present a variety of paintable architecture and offer splendid subjects for all sorts of mediums. I have in mind such well-known and impressive buildings as Edinburgh Castle dramatically situated high above the city (and when floodlit, appears to have its foundations in the celestial night sky). Carisbrook, Dover, Windsor, Conway, Harlech and Orgueil Castle in Jersey are further examples of well-preserved historic monuments.

There are others, however, not so familiar, perhaps on account of their lesser rank in lineage, which while failing to inspire romantic emotions are nevertheless deserving of a pictorial record. Two which I have in mind are castles in Warkworth, Northumberland, and St. Mawes, Cornwall. Compact in appearance and tucked away into the hillside, the castle at St. Mawes is in a remarkable state of preservation, due no doubt to its capitulation at the time of the Civil Wars. It is built at five levels and crowned on top by a squat round tower and in its typical Cornish surroundings makes a very attractive subject for a painting. From castles to abbeys and stately homes is no great step. Wiltshire, I would say, is particularly rich in fine manors and the like.

There is a splendid abbey at Malmesbury, another at Laycock (with its haunted stables), and these together with Rainsbury Manor, Heale House and St. Anne's at Salisbury come readily to mind. The temptation in such cases to approach too close to these stately buildings often robs them of their potential value as a focal point in a landscape. To give a few examples of the saying "where distance lends enchantment", *Harewood House* painted by Turner is relegated to a position in the middle distance and partially screened by a clump of trees. In his masterly painting of Hurstmonceux Castle, Turner has again pushed the building right back into the landscape. Constable adopted the same procedure when he painted Petworth House.

Three viewpoints of Windsor Castle

Cowdray Ruins. The importance of cast shadows in architectural subjects

Gateway, Hampton Court

Doorway, Guildford Cathedral

East Gate, Totnes

South Gate, King's Lynn

Roch Castle, Pembrokeshire

West Gate, Canterbury

The figures give a sense of height to this sketch of the ruins of Glastonbury Abbey

Rex Whistler did the same with his *Haddon Hall*, and in such paintings as *Newstead Abbey* by C. Varley, *Knowles* by Frederick de Cot, *Lord Burlington's Villa* by J. Rigaud, the artist in each case has adopted this long-distance view of the building and has scored by so doing. On the other hand, lovers of Elizabethan architecture may well be induced to take a closer view of such aristocratic and spacious examples as Melford and Kentwell Hall in Norfolk and Borwick Hall in Lancashire; the latter lending itself admirably for a detailed study because of the interesting welding together of the baronial and stately with the domestic portions of the building. But without an effective combination of light and shade, such tempting "close-ups" of Stowhead, Montacute and Corsham Court in Somerset would prove difficult to make pictorially acceptable.

Useful references from my sketch-book

36

As the reader will have remarked, there has been no intention of presenting him with any exact itinerary. No guide-book authority as to number or locality of such paintable subjects, for any such information is beyond the scope of this little book. But rather it has been my hope that by dropping a hint or a passing reference, the reader will be encouraged to take out his own map and together with his sketching kit make his own discoveries.

While man's ingenuity in building fine houses is far less apparent in many counties in Wales and Scotland, it is only because vast areas are still left as Nature intended. Carnarvonshire is said to be "without a sign of cattle, man, or any sign of the work of man". In Scotland there is certainly more of Nature's handiwork and less of the work of man. That is in no way meant to suggest, however, that either country is barren of picturesque rural architecture. In Wales there is to be found evidence of historic memorials, castles, abbeys and great houses, such as Conway, Beaumaris, Bere, Criccieth, Harlech and Flint, all built during the thirteenth century

Another aspect of Cowdray Ruins

St. Mawes Castle

and all fought over. The same number and variety of historic buildings apply beyond the borders into Scotland. Indeed, the wide open and mountainous prospects in both countries which meet the eye rarely present a view which does not contain some form of ancient or domestic architecture—nestling in a valley, precariously poised on the slope of a hill or standing as a sentinel, majestic or forlorn on the far-flung distant horizon.

Edinburgh Castle

Quick watercolour of Bamburgh Castle

Guernsey from Castle Carey

CHAPTER FIVE

Bridges

B RIDGES would surely provide enough material for a book
in itself, so many and varied are they in shape, size, material
and suitability of purpose. There are four main types of bridge—
beam, cantilever, suspension and arch, of which the last is the most
common. The lifting bridge and the swinging bridge are to be found
along our canals, and occasionally one meets with an old bridge
which has two or more cutwaters or recesses to form pedestrian
retreats when vehicles are encountered. All these types of bridges
are to be found all over the British Isles, and the majority of them
lend themselves to the consideration of the landscape painter, for
there are few man-made constructions more to be commended as a
pictorial feature than a bridge. From the medieval bridge—or the
primitive type of stepping-stones—the ever-changing material used
in its construction has provided an infinite variety of designs,
wrought in wood, stone, brick, iron and concrete (the last, alas, is
perhaps too much in evidence for lovers of the past tradition of
great bridge building). For like every other form of architecture, it
must be admitted that there are "bridges and bridges". Unfor-
tunately many of the most modern which span or carry our arterial
motorways, have little pictorial value—apart from severe simplicity
they serve their purpose and no more!

Mercifully there are still many bridges extant which serve both
purposes, being well built, completely functional and at the same
time are a delight to the eye. It is not generally recognized that often
our first encounter with a bridge is either walking over or driving
across it. We have no idea, unless it be a suspension bridge, with its
overhead construction, what it looks like. In short, what lies underneath. A good example of this is the famous Pulteney Bridge in
Bath. Being flanked by shops on either side we traverse its length
as we would along a short shopping street. Because we are on it
we cannot see it. It only proclaims its architectural features when
we get off the main thoroughfare and view it from the public

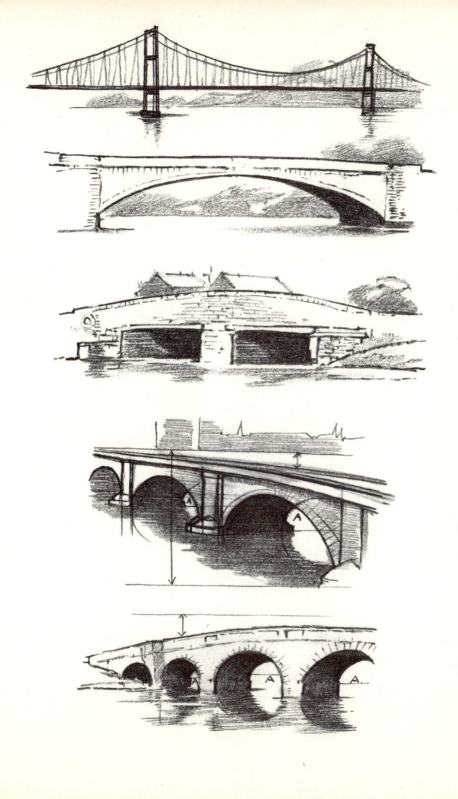

Low viewpoint of viaduct

Old and new at Pulborough, Sussex

Modern bridge under construction over the River Severn

gardens which flank the river which it spans. And it is only from this viewpoint that painters, including Sickert, have been able to record it for us.

Ancient bridges and those of historic antiquity naturally appeal to the artist, and in this respect mention must be made of several which one hopes will be preserved despite their obvious inadequacy for modern traffic. The medieval bridge over the Medway at Aylesford immediately comes to mind. The new bridge built higher up the river, not only solves the traffic problem but affords a view of the old bridge which allows its medieval structure to be appreciated to the full. The famous road bridge at Telford in Conway, Carnarvonshire, proving dangerous for modern traffic, one hopes will be retained on account of its pictorial value, especially as a new bridge has been built to carry the main road to Holyhead.

The famous iron bridge which gave its name to the town in Shropshire is also worthy of preservation, if for no other reason than to record as evidence of the early Industrial Revolution. (Though the fabric of the bridge is lacking some of its embellishments, the local authority, one reads, has undertaken to resurface the road and make the necessary restoration in the stone work.) At Warkworth, in Northumberland, a proposal is to widen the fourteenth-century bridge over the Coquet as it was admittedly inadequate for modern traffic, but as this widening would have radically altered the character of the bridge, already disfigured by the dislodgement of part of the parapet and the erection of wooden railings, an alternative proposal is to build a new bridge downstream, and if this is sited sufficiently far away from the old one, the beauty of it and its setting will be preserved.

There are over sixty bridges between Cricklade and Staines on the Thames, and one at Maidenhead, built in 1777, is a good example of one of the oldest and indeed most paintable.

Tuke Street and London Street, divided by the River Kanet, are joined by the High Bridge at Reading. This elegant steep little stone bridge was built in 1788, at, we are told, "considerable expense".

The western keystones of the three central arches of the bridge at Cardington on the Bedford–Biggleswade Road bear the following inscriptions—1st stone "J. Smeaton, Eng.", middle stone "S.W.

1778" and the third stone "S. Green, Surv."—so it might appear that three personages had a hand in its construction. Although of no great age, Ashberry Bridge on the edge of Scawton Moor, merits a second look, with its three semicircular arches; it is seen to be particoloured, being natural grey stone on the south side and red stained on the other.

Lady Bridge, at Wilcot in Wiltshire, is the result of private enterprise by the owner in order to preserve her estate which was divided by the canal. The ornamental arch, carved, rusticated and balustrated, make unusual features and show what variations are possible in imaginative bridge designing. The date is 1808, and recorded in an attractive painting by Vincent Lines.

So ancient is the Tarr Steps in Somerset that the makers had no word to describe its development from the primitive stepping-stone

crossing. Twenty rough piers, two or three feet above the stream, are protected by sloping breakwaters on the exposed side; along these piles are laid the blocks of flat stone which extend along the entire width, 180 feet, including the paved approaches.

Ethelbert White has painted a very pleasing watercolour of this bridge which must be the oldest in the country, unhappily it must be said, in a state of sad dilapidation. The famous five-arched bridge at Henley on the Thames prompted Horace Walpole to write: "There is not a sight in the island more worthy of being visited." Certainly the view from Atlacts Wharf, showing the bridge, the old Angel Hotel and the fifteenth-century tower of St. Mary's Church makes an admirable painting by W. Fairclough. A six-arched bridge and the oldest one over the Wye River in Hereford dates back to 1400, and four of its arches belong to that period. The bridge and its setting from all angles is a favourite one with artists.

The hump-backed bridge belongs to a type common in many counties and wherever old canals wander—a good example is to be found in the Basin at Stourport.

Pulteney Bridge, Bath, Somerset

The Glory Hole Bridge, Lincoln

There are a pair of massive cutwaters in the sixteenth-century bridge at Bridgsend, Wales; only two arches, spanning a distance of 27 yards, are now visible, these are segmented in shape and it would appear that there was very little traffic in those days, for the bridge is steep, slippery with cobbles and only wide enough for very small vehicles to pass each other.

An attractive private bridge, but now open to the public, is the small seventeenth-century steep and (stepped up each side) stone balustraded bridge spanning a sunken road at York House, Twickenham.

No brief account of our bridges in the United Kingdom can exclude a mention of the famous bridge at Gretna. Here Cotman immortalized it and many subsequent painters have featured it in their pictures. The balustrade was removed in 1789, is now, I believe, replaced, so that this handsome single-arched bridge remains as pictorially attractive as it proved when it was first erected. Another famous bridge, the Suspension Bridge at Clifton, is noteworthy only on the account of it being pictorially impossible owing to its great height above the river.

47

Indeed for the purpose of this book, it is perhaps more with the problem of how to draw and introduce a bridge into our landscape rather than with their historic significance, although it is often a question of their age and period features that first attract our attention.

Bridges, let me say at once, are not all that easy to draw. Unless proportion is observed their stability is threatened. I have seen drawings of bridges that would scarcely support a sparrow, let alone a human being or a vehicle of any kind. See that the distance between the keystone of the arch (or arches) and the parapet is deep enough to sustain the weight that it is built to carry. See also that the arch (or arches) are firmly drawn in an uninterrupted curve and the thickness diminishes as it ascends to its apex. Although these points should be obvious when drawing on the spot they are often at fault when drawn from memory. It will be found that most bridges are improved pictorially when seen in perspective, i.e. not full face. Here a proper regard for diminishing height, length and width in its proportion is all important. And look closely at the juncture at either end where the bridge meets the opposing river bank, for in most cases the level of a bridge is continued on a horizontal plane throughout. It is rather a welcome exception than the rule when the road mounts and descends on either side, as in the pack bridge. Any assistance offered by light and shade with their

Hammersmith Bridge

"Port Sunlight"—crayon drawing

Abstract treatment of a town—tinted with coloured pencil

resultant cast shadows must also be utilized if our bridge is to resemble a solid structure. The effect of lighting, its strength and direction, will also determine the degree of tone of its reflection in the river and only at first hand is it possible to assess the extent of its clarity of reproduction according to time of day, weather conditions and viewpoint. And all this, for the reason that there are no rigid rules for our guidance which cannot be upset in certain cases dependent on conditions mentioned above, and illustrated in the text.

Moreover, when a bridge spans a *road* similar anomalies can obtain, the difference being that in normal conditions on a solid surface, it is the shadow under the arch and not its reflection which affects the tone of the road, except after heavy rain when it may well reflect the image of the bridge as surely as if it were a transparent surface. Some bridges are seen to gain pictorially at a distance, great enough to include their entire length, which can then be used as a line of repose in the middle distance of our landscape and connecting two opposing forms—and on which the eye can rest. Others are seen to possess architectural features to justify a portrait rather than an item in the composition, in which case a detailed study is required. I have given examples among the illustrations from my own sketch-books and can heartily recommend this practice of collecting first-hand reference. It is of great value for future paintings where a bridge is wanted which has the authentic ring about it.

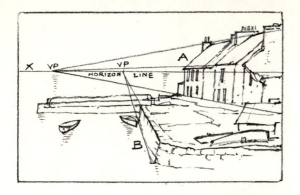

Here there are two vanishing points—A + B—on the horizon line X, both inside the picture

CHAPTER SIX

Viewpoint and Perspective

A LANDSCAPE, if we accept the dictionary definition, is simply "a piece of inland scenery", but, as we have seen, to the landscape painter it is usually a view of the countryside in which some architectural feature appears.

On the other hand, the architectural matter sometimes becomes the main part of the picture, as in a market place, a city square or some main thoroughfare, and when this happens such a painting falls more logically under the heading of a "townscape" as the scene is composed of buildings to the exclusion of any Nature forms.

I propose therefore to include both kinds of picture for discussion as the latter forms quite a large proportion of our outdoor painting and comprises the majority of illustrations in travel books, in comparison with those of a purely rural aspect of the countryside.

One vanishing point X as all the houses and road are at right angles to the horizon line

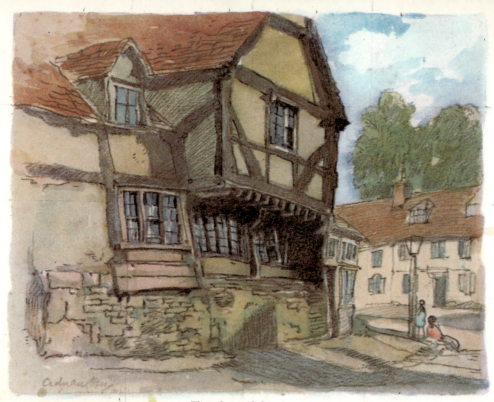

Tinted pencil drawing

Church and Houses

A distant view of a town or village is one thing, a close-up of a
street scene where there is no hedge-row, tree or stream to vary the
composition, is quite another. Our problem here is the choice of
the best vantage-point so that a sufficient assortment of shape and
sizes of building is obtained. For instance we can look up and down
our street or look up or down at some house or group of houses.
Viewing a particular building from one side or the other often
reveals a more attractive aspect than when it directly faces us.
(Portrait painters often choose a three-quarter view of their sitter
rather than a full face.) It is here, with something akin to reluctance,
that I venture to introduce the subject of perspective. Now there
are students (I was one) who are lucky enough to have a natural
perspective, but some I know find it very difficult. Others dismiss
it out of hand as an outmoded convention which emasculates
enterprise and cramps imagination.

But where architecture in landscape is in question, I cannot view
it as a hindrance but rather as a help. For what is more necessary for
portraying any building as a solid body, i.e. having depth as well as
height and width, or in rendering a street scene so that it advances

Another example where the vanishing point of the line of cottages is outside the picture.

Palace of Holyrood House

or recedes, than that provided by the simple rules of perspective? The word itself, *per*: "through", *specio*: "I see", is simple enough. It certainly must not be confused with a specialized form of drawing executed by a specialist draughtsman. Neither is an architectural training necessary for its attainment. Mathematics need not come into it. In one way the painter of architectural subjects is no more worse off than the figure painter who has had no training in surgical anatomy. Both, however, should have a desire to know something about how a figure works, or in this case, something about the construction of a building and its period. It helps when he comes to draw or paint it.

Now, any sort of detached house or building has four sides and unless we stand directly in front of it, we see a second wall—in perspective, i.e. it is seen to decrease in height and width. Although the far end of the side wall is as tall as the front, it *appears* to be shorter. The greater the depth of the house, the shorter it looks.

It is foolhardy to refuse the evidence of our eyes, for when all is said and written about geometric perspective, it is just how we all see everything. Once that is accepted, it is only a question of

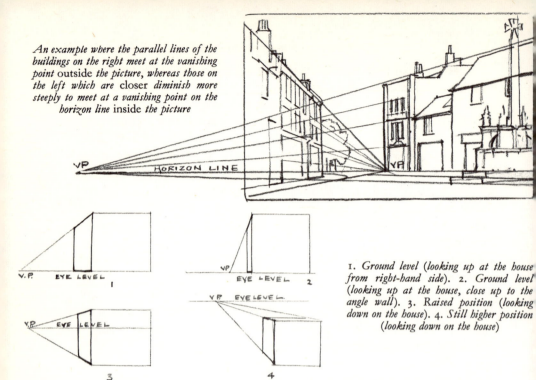

An example where the parallel lines of the buildings on the right meet at the vanishing point outside *the picture, whereas those on the left which are* closer *diminish more steeply to meet at a vanishing point on the* horizon line *inside the picture*

1. *Ground level (looking up at the house from right-hand side).* 2. *Ground level (looking up at the house, close up to the angle wall).* 3. *Raised position (looking down on the house).* 4. *Still higher position (looking down on the house)*

drawing what we see accurately! And if the few following guiding principles are understood, perspective is robbed of its terror. For instance, we all know (or should know) that parallel lines, if extended to the horizon will be seen to meet at a point called the vanishing point. Looking down any straight road or railway track will prove that!

Therefore, the top and bottom of a house which are parallel to each other, together with the top and bottom of all its windows and doors, will, if extended to the horizon, also meet. All we have to decide is where this horizon line is to be drawn, for this line is always at eye-level, whether we stand, sit or lie on the ground. All parallel lines from wherever we draw them must meet on this line, but not necessarily at the same point. Now the point of sight is the point in a picture exactly opposite the eye of the beholder and is always situated somewhere on the line of the horizon. The height of this horizontal line and therefore of the point of sight is dependent on the height from which the spectator is supposed to take his observation. The horizontal line varies according to the height of the eye.

In drawing any scene from Nature, it will be seen that this line always maintains the same level as the eye of the painter. For example, if he takes a view standing on level ground, the horizon will appear low and the ground plane will be limited. If, on the other hand, the standpoint is from any considerable elevation, then the horizon will be higher and a wider range of the scene will be visible, and from still a greater height, such as from the top of a hill, the horizon still maintains its level with the spectator and the field of vision is that much more extended.

In passing, if when looking at any view through a window, we drew with paint on the surface of the glass all the lines of the objects we saw would constitute a true perspective representation of the scene. Thus it can be proved that we all see everything in Nature in terms of perspective.

Nothing, I believe, need concern us further than the application of these few rules, for by them any building or street scene from any viewpoint from which we elect to draw it will look exactly as we see it in Nature. If, on the other hand, the reader does not wish to convey a realistic solidity in his painting, this chapter will have no message for him. All I can say is that one cannot decide on the merits of perspective until they have been demonstrated and proved in practice.

I hope the accompanying diagrams will help to explain the text and support this claim.

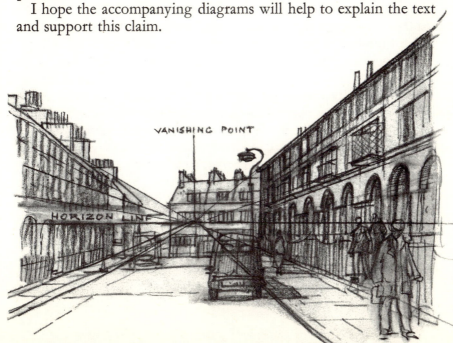

VANISHING POINT

HORIZON LINE

CHAPTER SEVEN

Drawing: Proportion, Selection, Balance and Detail

"I CANNOT draw a straight line!" The feared inability to execute this movement is much more understandable when a house or any building is under discussion. For whatever one has against straight lines as such, they are really very necessary in this case! Without a ruler they can be quite difficult. But unless we are depicting one of the latest steel and concrete box-like structures which are rearing their soulless bodies into the air in so many of our cities and towns, the mechanical ruled line is quite unnecessary. Perpendiculars we must have and they should be vertical! I know this because unless I watch out, my own free-hand uprights have a tendency to incline to the right! If such a slant is not checked when the initial construction lines are drawn in, your house, church, castle or ruin may appear to be about to collapse and this can be very frustrating if all the completed details have the same slant! To obviate this a single perpendicular *faintly ruled line* down the centre of your paper or close to where your proposed building is to be drawn, will act as a steadier for all your free-hand upright lines (and, of course, this guide line can be erased when it has done its job!).

This difficulty out of the way, our next problem is proportion. The actual drawing of buildings, especially those that are embellished with a mass of architectural detail, often present a formidable task to the beginner (and may I add for his comfort, are no easy problem to resolve for the professional artist, as I know!).

Just as in drawing trees the multitudinous number of separate leaves, if attempted in detail, rob the tree of its fundamental form and character, so the form and solidity of many types of building may well be lost in a mass of detail. It is the old story of the particular swamping the general.

And in order to surmount this difficulty the all-over mass must be

Pictorial possibilities of the industrial development

*Some straight lines and perpendiculars
in architectural subjects*

stated first—its height and width, the *shape* it makes! With half-closed eyes one can see these proportions far more clearly and the temptation to include all the inside decoration will not arise. I know how easy it is to follow particular features and become so engrossed with each bit of adjacent detail that you find that the parts are too great for the whole! Even when proportion has been stated correctly, surface detail may, in some cases, have to be suggested or even eliminated entirely, to preserve pictorial truth against factual accuracy. Now, what is actually implied by the word *proportion*? I make no apology for quoting in full one of Ruskin's penetrating aphorisms, because when he discusses the true meaning of proportion, what he writes is as applicable to the problem of the painter as that of the architect.

". . . whenever Proportion exists at all, one member of the composition must be either larger than, or in some way supreme over the rest. There is no proportion between equal things. They

can have symmetry only, and symmetry without proportion is not composition. . . . Any succession of equal things is agreeable, but to compose is to arrange unequal things and the first thing to be done in beginning a composition is to determine which is to be the principal thing." And further on, Ruskin sums up: "Have one large thing and several smaller things or one principal thing and several inferior things, and *bind them well together*." This is all so very true whether we are designing a building or composing a picture—and especially is it apposite when we are painting a picture with an architectural motif. And so is this, "Knock down a couple of pinnacles at either end of King's College Chapel and you will have a kind of proportion instantly." And again, "The moment the towers rise so high as to overpower the body and centre and become themselves the principal masses, they will destroy proportion unless they are made unequal and one of them the leading feature of the building." And finally, "But, in all events, get rid of equality, leave that to children and their *card houses*, the laws of nature are against it, in Arts as in politics."

And, of course, this incidentally is the reason why the majority of new public buildings look so monstrously wrong and impossible to integrate into our landscape painting. To view them in our countryside as they rise box upon box with a ruthless disregard for anything but efficiency for purpose is to realize the truth of these prophetic words of Ruskin.

In drawing a house (windmill, bridge, etc.) one has to arrange

these unequal things, and to determine which is to be the principal feature must be the first of our considerations. To compare the length of a bridge with its height from the surface of the water is more important to start with than the number of its arches. It is exactly the same with the building which has one tower or two. The height and width must be established first before you draw in the windows and doors. Again Ruskin is worth quoting when he warns us: "In fine west fronts with a pediment and two towers, the centre is always the principal mass, both in bulk and interest (as having the main gateway) and the towers are subordinate to it, as an animal's horns are to its head." And this rule will be seen to apply to the smallest detail as well as to the leading features.

If this lesson is well learnt, the student will never find that there is no room for that fourth window or chimney stack or pillar! There are many students I have met who, while capable of making a fairly accurate study of an isolated building, find some difficulty in drawing the same form in scale with the proportions of its intended setting. The chosen feature may be situated in the middle distance and yet when they come to introduce it, the proportions get out of hand and suddenly they find that the house, cottage or whatever it is, is threatening to occupy far too much of their picture and in consequence there is much rubbing out before the right balance is effected.

One way of obviating this is to draw in the landscape first and then it will be seen exactly where and what space the architectural form should occupy. Scale then is of major importance, if our landscape is not to be swamped with an architectural octopus— intended originally to be but a minor incident in the scene. Especially is this warning applicable to some decorated buildings, such as a castle or cathedral, studded with mullion windows, festooned with turrets and flanked with flying buttresses. Obsessional interest in these details will inevitably cause the edifice to grow and dwarf its surroundings. And, incidentally, it is only when we are engaged on sorting out with our pencils and sketch-books the suitable styles of building for our purpose—their order and period peculiarities— that our powers of discrimination and selection are brought to bear, and architectural anachronisms do not occur. And remembering above all if I may dare to repeat that in elaboration of detail we will

assuredly fall into the old sophistry of "the grains of corn and the heap".

THE VALUE OF A DISTANT FEATURE AND DRAWING DETAILS

While every county in the British Isles has its quota of architectural features, it must be admitted that there are many areas, especially in the Midlands, where roads cut through slabs of flat agricultural land on either side of which the eye searches in vain for any perpendicular (apart from an occasional clump of trees) to break the monotony of the horizonal plane. Miles of such country are to be found for example in Hertford, Cambridge and parts of Norfolk. But just as one has given up all hope of a break in the landscape, there can suddenly appear a distant church spire, a forlorn or derelict windmill, a welcome ruin and, at once, the bleak prospect is transformed into an attractive low horizon subject. And it is when this happens that the form, whatever shape the structure takes (and however distant), is found to be all-sufficient for our purpose. It is the *silhouette* it makes and not its *detail*. Indeed it is its very starkness, its isolation in the empty landscape that makes it such a dramatic incident. And to enhance this effect a simple sky is more effective than one in which clouds might lessen the required impact. For contrast is essential if the proper balance is to be achieved. All must be kept subservient to the focal point of interest, especially if it is situated on the skyline. So we see that proportion plays a major part when and wherever any architectural form is introduced into our landscape.

At this stage some technical hints (not rules, please note) might be of service to the beginner, especially when it applies to drawing details. Take windows first. It is advisable to strengthen the tone at the top of the window. If it is situated directly under the eaves there will be an obvious band of tone across the upper panes of glass. In contrast to this, the shadow under the windowsill should be lighter in tone, thus obviating the danger of making the window stand away from the face of the building.

Windows should always be regarded as holes in the wall, that is to say, darker in tone than the surrounding stone or brick work. Only at night when the room is illuminated inside does the reverse apply. The tone of cottage windows which are divided up into small sections should be light enough for the pencilling in of necessary detail to show up. And all such detail, ornament, porticoes, gables, pediments, etc., especially in cathedrals and great houses, must be governed by the scale of the building. At a distance these decorations need only suggesting, but the suggestions, the touching in, must be precise, and there must be no fumbling, especially if a pen is employed.

In portraying old buildings there is a danger of adopting a formula of "broken lines", so insistently advocated by past teachers. Certainly the broken line is useful in the right places but if no precise line appears anywhere, the dignity of old age will give place to undignified dotage—all will appear to be crumbling away and that will only result in a weak drawing.

In the representation of tiling on a roof, the broken line is legitimate, but only if used with discrimination, otherwise, the same disintegration will result as mentioned above.

The same controlled technique applies to any expanse of brick wall, the surface of which would prove monotonous if all the lines and divisions of brick work were laboriously drawn in. Indeed, in

Palladian Bridge—Wiltshire

Iron Bridge—Shropshire

some portions of both roof and wall area, intervals should be left blank to obviate the overcrowding of such detail. I hope that a glance at some of my examples will show what can be achieved by these technical devices—for this, admittedly, is what they are!

Always seize upon any shadows which may occur on the building especially those thrown by chimney-stacks onto a roof. The pattern they make help to break up a large surface of tiles, slates or brick-work. The same use can be made of deep shadows thrown by an overhanging thatch or roof on a whitewashed wall, just as a more precise shadow of an open casement window can decorate a similar surface of the outside fabric.

In these days when practically every house is decorated (if that is the word) by a television mast, a question arises as to whether or not it is artistically legitimate to add them in the outline of the chimney-stacks. I find that against an evening sky the new design they make can be very attractive, but once again it must be a matter of dis-crimination what use one makes of them and when to leave them out. Where a group of buildings are in deep tone, these delicate skeleton masts can act as pictorially as the delicate tracery of the top-most branches and twigs in a clump of trees. Neither intimacy nor familiarity should blur our observation where such visual details are concerned.

Finally I would say that over-conscientiousness lies at the root of the trouble with most students. Putting in too much detail (a fault we have all shared in at some time or another) is a special temptation when drawing some building of great historic and architectural interest, and it is only as a producer and not as an announcer that by "artful" suggestion we can in full confidence leave the beholder to "furnish" the necessary details and thus add to his enjoyment of the picture. Sir Charles Holmes sums up the aim when he says: "Lastly we may note how the use of black and white, of firm pencil touches alternating everywhere with the sparkle of the white paper, between them contribute to the vibrancy of tone, and herewith to the general vitality of the result."

And this result of richness of content can be reached without a heaviness of general tonality. These hints apply of course to drawing in pen, pencil or chalk. For these techniques are largely a matter of significant touches, pictorial articulations, if you like, and must be in the end sorted out and applied in as personal a manner as possible.

CHAPTER EIGHT

Painting: Various Techniques

ALTHOUGH sound drawing must be a requisite in the paint-ing of architecture in the oil medium, exactness of detail must not rob the building of its solidarity. This, of course, does not imply a ruthless elimination of all decoration with which the building may be embellished, as this would turn a palace into a prison and a domestic dwelling into a primitive cave and a Gothic church into an urban chapel! But it must be taken as a warning in case the conscientious following of every minute feature overlays the funda-mental construction and impairs characteristics underlying the details of its façade.

Colour and tone—recessional values—contrast in light and shade —all these painter-like properties must be our first concern. These have always been and always will be the overall considerations when we use such a plastic medium as oils. In watercolours— especially the watercolour drawing—the sacrifice of surface decora-tion does not apply, not in the same way, except in as much as suggestion may often have to be employed instead of precise repre-sentation. In any case the scaffolding of a watercolour, that is the drawing, is fixed before the colour washes are applied, while in an oil painting, construction lines are sufficient to establish the form, and the detail is added with the brush—and just how much detail is introduced becomes the problem indicated above. I would rather have the impressive dignity by which our eyes are first attracted to a noble house, palace or church, than to have the issue confused with a multitude of parts, meticulously catalogued and overcharged with architectural meaning. Such decoration must be made to keep its place, to be sensed rather than seen. As long as firm drawing guides our painting hand, a sure sweep of the brush well loaded with the right colour will more than recompense for the necessary subjection or even obliteration of any minutia devised by the hand of an architect!

Colour and tone and the rendering of solid form are worth any amount of fastidious elaboration. Just as long as—and this must be repeated—the character of the edifice remains inviolate. Look at the paintings of Turner, Cézanne, Vlaminck, Utrillo and Van Gogh, for they offer all the support for bigness of handling in obedience to architectural requirements. Their buildings, inns, churches, bridges, are so real—authentic and so unfussed, so endurable. For it is well to remember that just when the Impressionists were in danger of caressing the shadow on the wall, Cézanne restored the balance by reintroducing the solidity of the wall on which the shadow but casts its transitory pattern—which is the right way round when portraying architecture in any form.

Nature's colouring often discolours—or beautifies, the surface of walls, doors or roofs of buildings. At the same time the fabric may have its own local colour—sandstone, granite, brick, timber— and these surfaces, especially those of wood, may themselves be painted by the hand of man a distinctive hue. Now there is a danger of copying this particular shade of colour and by so doing causing a discord with Nature's surroundings. Blue-green shutters can clash with the ivy-clad surrounding of the window. I would say that bright major tints—such as scarlet, royal blue or daffodil yellow, if they occur on a house or farm building, should be discreetly toned down by adding a touch of black with each colour. The temptation to work from a colour photograph of some building, strongly lit with dramatic shadows and, furthermore, all the visible detailed features at your service already translated on a two-dimensional surface, appears to some eager but lazy painters too strong to resist. To the present reader, I would whisper—it's an easy way round, the result is never completely "you", because you have merely copied what another eye has registered and that eye is the mechanical lens of a camera. There is still no substitute for "I was there".

To some reader avid for a specific method in oils that produces a robust finish of extremely vigorous brushwork, I can do no better than quote Myerscough-Walker when he examines a painting of an abbey or church "where certain passages will appear very recessive, certain textures of stone work in the distance very subtle and the fine white lines of the courses of stonework almost too fine for paint. One wonders how such a variety of effects and surfaces is possible in thick oil paints. If, however, under the paint there is a

Tinted ink drawing of Old House, Rye

thick white ground brushed on very vigorously in an almost plaster-like consistency—allowed to dry and then sandpapered—there will be, before painting is started, a very rich texture containing robust brushmarks. This may be covered with a *thin* layer of paint the colour of the background and rubbed with the fingers. While wet, certain parts are scraped away to leave a mottled texture, and lines are drawn with a scalpel to show the dead white ground. Thus one has a tone drawing of the subject giving the appearance of thick and vigorous paintwork."

Nevertheless, he writes later, "the technique of any painting is a reflection of the period in which it was painted . . . each age has to express itself in its own way and each finds a technique peculiar to itself . . . different from any that has preceded it".

The technique of other mediums, such as watercolour, pen or chalk and wash, coloured pencils, etc., apply equally well to the topographical representation of Nature whether treated with precision or handled loosely according to the subject matter and the painter's personal approach.

Impressionistic treatment in line and wash of Oasthouse

Key drawing from railway bridge in North London

In watercolours, I should say that the drawing, i.e. definition of architectural details, should not be obscured by opaque colour. The washes should be transparent so that underlying touches with pencil, pen or chalk, suffice for the required accents. In swifter impressions these controlled gestures by which the colour is applied and which denote the various changes of tints in the surface texture of the building should be laid on and left untouched. Although a small brush is necessary when small areas are to be painted, such as a door, a pediment or a pillar, this does not imply a number of tentative touches, but one single deft stroke with a confident hand.

Overworked paintings, especially in watercolour, instead of rendering the building more solid in texture, have the opposite effect, and if the colour be sweet, something suspiciously like a piece of coloured confectionery will result.

Colour, Character and Perspective

Wash drawing of Shoreham Cement Works, Sussex

CHAPTER NINE

Additional Material

COMPILING appropriate material for a book of this nature has disclosed many gaps in the sketch-books which I devote to the collection of useful and unusual forms of rural architecture. By diligent inquiry I have endeavoured to remedy these omissions, making special journeys to hunt down such features as windmills, watermills, oasthouses and dovecots, etc. Sometimes the excursions have proved abortive as when recently despatched to a famous windmill, last seen some years ago, I found on my arrival that the mill had been demolished to make room for a garage! And surely in a very few cases can a filling-station be said to recompense the artist in his quest for some ancient structure which in the past beautified the spot.

Windmills in particular, I have found, are becoming collectors' pieces. Once there were as many as forty windmills on the heights round Rochester. By 1883 the number had dropped to twenty-four. By 1930 only one remained and that disappeared in 1947. When run to earth they are often discovered to be but broken relics of their former decorative and useful selves. And only as long as the worn-out, the derelict and disused mill be considered a picturesque feature of the landscape, is it worth the students' time and trouble to locate its whereabouts. I am reminded, however, that there is a movement afoot, whereby enlightened authorities are restoring some famous mills, and though they will no longer function as of old they are being put in working order to be preserved as ancient monuments. This is heartening because a windmill is unlike any other piece of agricultural architecture, the machinery being enclosed by a circular or hexagonal body at the top of which the four skeletonal arms gesticulate with dramatic effect. Such unique silhouettes have figured in many famous paintings of the past. Constable, Turner, Cotman, Crome, Harding and the Impressionists have all

Terrick Mill. Pencil sketch

*Terrick Mill. Line and wash sketch
(see finished subject in colour on page 27)*

Toll House

More leaves from the artist's sketch-book

75

handed down landscapes in which the windmill makes an ideal focal point in the composition. Watermills, on the other hand, though threatened by modern devices for utilizing water's power, are more numerous and easier to locate. Immediately one thinks of Flatford Mill which John Constable immortalized in 1817 and which today is still standing as the original memorial to his great painting. I have chosen the ancient watermill at Terrick in Sussex to illustrate the usefulness of making roughs before deciding which view makes the best composition. I generally find that my first sketch is the most obvious and hackneyed, and it is generally discarded in favour of a subsequent drawing, taken from a less frequented position. I have numbered the three reproduced in order of my preference. Some of these mills achieve a rare dignity with their lofty timbered walls, massive stone foundations and adjacent great wheel, remorselessly threshing and churning the dark turbulent water into a sparkling cascade of translucent foam.

The North Mill at Midhurst (here illustrated), although only portrayable from certain positions, and then only when the surrounding trees are bare of leaves to disclose its grey-green walls, pierced with blind dusty windows, makes a worthy subject for both oil and watercolour mediums. Among other watermills which have distinguishing characteristics in outline and construction, mention should be made of Newark Mill at Ripley with its massive sloping roofs; the watermill at Houghton with similar perpendicular features, the Mill at Hambledon, strictly horizontal in design and full of windows, and that at Colchester with its mellow colouring and long fenced approach, all having a water foundation in which their tiled roofs and timbered sides are duly reflected. An old watermill that can claim the distinction of being on an island site can be found on the River Wey at Byfleet. Here the timbered Mill House, which is early Georgian, stands between a small stream and the main river.

Less distinguished in appearance and for that reason easier to be overlooked are the remaining Toll Houses or Turnpike cottages, which crouch close to the verge of certain of our country roads. Squat in appearance with their low watchful windows on the lookout for the approaching traffic, they add their pictorial offering as does the prim compact lodge which guards the entrance to many a

North Mill, Midhurst, Sussex

Newark Mill, Ripley, Surrey

Mill at Hembledon, Sussex

stately home of England, in the grounds of which may be found follies, such as classic temples, gothic ruins and observatories of pseudo-medieval design. These, together with the varied handsome wrought-iron gates, their flanking pillars of brick or stone, surmounted by massive stone urns or heraldic animals, which mark the entrance of their drives, are all deserving of a sketch. Although often unrecognized through ignorance of the original function for which they were erected, the dovecot provides a sizeable and picturesque design. Rare though they are in England, it is in Scotland and in East Lothian particularly, that the dovecot can be said to form a part of the countryside in which many fine examples are to be found. It must be admitted, however, that the majority of these have passed their period of intensive use, and of those remaining, many have lost their nests or lanterns and are only fit to be used for storage or other farm purposes. The "beehive", so named because of its shape, is said to be the earliest, dating back to the sixteenth century. The "lectern" "square", "octagonal" and "cylindrical" designs belong to the eighteenth and nineteenth centuries. A typical example has massive walls tapering up to a flat-domed roof, covered with stone slabs and with a circular opening in the centre through which the pigeons used to fly. The walls are constructed with rubble, generally roughcast and often whitewashed. Round holes or slits do duty for windows and ventilation and the small door is always situated on the southerly side. With or without their pigeons, these robust and distinctive structures should always be welcome to the artist with a sketch-book. Indeed all such buildings should be noted for further use, for is that not what our sketch-books are for—and in the finding of which makes our search for new subjects so rewarding?

Conclusion

"THE face of Britain", to quote from a recent leader in *The Times*, "is being changed and threatened with more change at a greater speed and on a larger scale than at any time at least since the Industrial Revolution. New arterial and lesser roads and road widening have brought about transformation scenes, often distressing, all over the country and their impact is only beginning to be felt." (Landscape painters are all too aware of this.) "Valleys and villages have been swallowed up to satisfy the ever-growing demand for water, and others will be doomed to submersion. Cities, market towns and villages are being pulled about so drastically that their old inhabitants would scarcely recognize them. Indeed, the urban dweller (and the artist, may I add) proud of the traditional beauty of our street patterns and buildings at their best, may well view the future with despair."

But if these questions are addressed to some landscape painters, are not some of us guilty, perhaps, of too much championing of picturesque survivals of rural architecture "set in quaint twisting lanes and alley ways"? Is there not a danger of preserving the "olde worlde" atmosphere in our paintings and defending too hotly our cherished landmarks in our landscapes? That may well be but let me put it another way. How far can Nature contain the growing invasion of factories, power plants, petrol stations, road widening and the menace of the pylon network across the countryside, not to mention car parks and aerodromes, and still offer the painter sufficient pictorial elbow-room to compose his naturalistic pictures? In face of what has already been accomplished or destroyed, I consider the question as valid and one of vital importance to the artist and student. It would seem that he can either leave out or turn a blind eye to the octopus of modern architectural forms, or endeavour to integrate these new landmarks into his future landscapes. For there is no doubt that all these modern man-made constructions will in time be accepted and one supposes at some future date will even be cherished with nostalgic affection! Certain it is better to meet this challenge of the changing face of Britain and with skill and artistic judgment come to painter-like terms with what may at first sight appear repugnant, but on second sight be found an acceptable—even indispensable—feature in many contemporary aspects of our present and future landscape.

The essential difference between the old and the new is that old architecture still appears to have a closer relationship with its environment by increasing the sense of locality, whereas the latter still appears as a foreign intrusion. While this is understandable, it must not prejudice and blind the eye to the artistic possibilities of reconciling these two warring factors and make them to co-exist side by side in pictorial harmony. One is almost tempted to believe that a continual war of attrition has always been waged between the defending forces of Nature's soil and the persistent infiltration of architecture into her domain. And despite the efforts to dislodge the man-made edifice, despite the ruthless ravages of storm, hurricane, flood and decay, the building meets the challenge and by its power of endurance actually beautifies the territory of her implacable enemy!

And just as Nature has been seen to assimilate the foreign architectural body, so I verily believe that many modern buildings will settle down pictorially into the landscape, and as I have hinted above, who knows in years to come even the resented pylon will be relegated to an ancient monument and carefully preserved as a picturesque relic for a future generation of painters to record with affectionate regard and possible regret!

In the meantime I hope I have demonstrated that there is still an abundant variety of rural architecture still available and waiting to be immortalized by our pencils and paints.